SIDE NOTES OF
GROWING UP

by Benjamin Hinamanu

Chapbook Press

Chapbook Press
Schuler Books
2660 28th Street SE
Grand Rapids, MI 49512
(616) 942-7330
www.schulerbooks.com

Printed at Schuler Books in Grand Rapids, MI,
on the Espresso Book Machine®

Library of Congress Control Number: in file

ISBN 13: 9781936243808
ISBN 10: 1936243806

© Benjamin Hinamanu, 2014

DEDICATED TO all the moments in
my life I've been so angry that I've said
the wrong things to the right people.

ACCEPTING
CHALLENGES

IT ALL BEGAN HERE.

chapter one

As a child I remember walking everywhere. We had no car, and pride usually trumped asking for a ride home. The long walk to the grocery store turned into a longer walk home with all we could carry in our arms. *I used to think learning and living were the same thing.* Knowledge was so important to me because I wouldn't have to mentally complain about carrying the groceries if I could understand the purpose of my sweat.

See I was angry, I was angry not because I was lazy, I was angry because the kids in my class never understood carrying the groceries home. See I was angry back then, but I was wrong. Instead of comparing my problems to others I should have been comparing my problems to the problem, my lack of hard work.

The groceries started getting less heavy. I started grabbing more bags. See instead of looking at it as a chore, I looked at it as a challenge. We're getting home with these groceries and I don't care how far we have to walk.

HIDDEN
BIRTHDAYS

Growing up and growing old used to mean the same thing to me. Never really saw the point in life because as a kid I couldn't afford pencils and felt like I was dying to live. That constant struggle to want for others what they wanted for me buried me in a pit of emotion. Alone and Uninspired made Anger and Isolation an easy place to run to.

CONSIDERED
WEIRDNESS

chapter three

Weird how memories and time sometimes blend and create confusion .

Weird how one only misses something when someone has that something.

Weird how 17 billion dollars and 17 seconds feel the same to some people.

Weird how pedestrians watch where they walk, but never talk to those who sit.

Weird how kissing a girl and finding the world sometimes feel similar.

Weird how going to sleep and waking up can turn into the opposite.

———————————

Weird how believing in onesself means somebody already joined that team.

GENERATIONS
HELPING

HURTING GENERATIONS

It scares me to think about the state of our future. I mean we have some girls claiming Valencia is the perfect "natural", and NFL + NBA players unable to spell the word "resources". No wonder we ignore global warming; we care more about Tinder than tidal waves from melting glaciers. People show more interest in Bieber's drunk driving than Benghazi getting bombed. People will stare and make comments if the people holding hands aren't the "right" color, gender, height, education level, or size but yet, not blink an eye when the murder rate in Chicago goes up 50% in a summer (most victims being kids ages 16-24).

It scares me to think that the United States leads the world in defense spending but yet there are places in Compton & Flint that I can't walk around.

It scares me to think how our society has become a melting pot of immigrants while also becoming a melting pot of ignorance. Beyond Democratic vs Republican, issues like empathy & understanding need to be talked about. We might not all agree on issues like abortion, gay marriage & nuclear weapons but don't we HAVE to agree on things such as child/sex slavery ending, the crime rate lowering & living healthier lives?

All of these things scare me, yet inspire me. Fear inspiring action.

SORRY,
THANK YOU.

As I grow up I have been learning the importance of an apology. Apologies are easy. Forgiveness, on the other hand, extraordinarily difficult. Apologies make the abuser feel better, forgiveness allows the victim to move forward.

TEACH ME HOW
TO BE TAUGHT

In 2014 public education still confuses me. The concept of sitting in a class full of relatively all strangers to be educated about a mass produced subject seems stupid. That's like taking 30 different seeds from plants putting them all under 100 degree weather and expecting all of them to ripen in 2 weeks. That kind of organized pressure leads to kids cheating. They cheat because their understanding of our educational system becomes honest.

Society values a grade over learning. Society values memorizing the information over creative responses to outside understanding. Simply think that we all learn differently and once public schools stop mass producing the question, students will start mass producing more solutions.

FINDING
HER.

chapter seven

Being in love is real. I never really understood
that. It took me 20 years to prioritize my emotions
enough to care for a girl as much as she cared
for me. It's complicated. You have that phase
where you're sexually attracted to her; that phase
is smooth, and it should be understood in 3-5
seconds. Once that phase is over, the mentally
attractive phase begins. The first conversation you
both have can be considered almost as important
as her name. Once you get passed that phase you
dip into the trend of mass texting each other
daily hoping that new information or emotions
will sprout from a new iMessage. This is quickly
followed by that mixed time you're "talking".
Not "talking" as in verbally talking, but as in
you and your significant other are up on deck in
the batting cage called 'love,' and nobody should
interfere with your possible home run.

Its socially insane, but its real. It's somebody
adding to your life randomly not because they
want something but because they have you. Love
teaches us about getting something for yourself
but also getting her on a deeper level. Love is
about finding each other in other things when
you're away. Love is like a stranger force feeding
you a random flavored milk shake.

You're scared because you've not known the person long enough to trust them. Terrified because the flavor could be anything, but it ends up being so delicious that it's the only milkshake acceptable to drink now. Love creates strength.

& karma is real. Be careful.

#NEVERFORGETMUFASA

chapter eight

<u>Casually finding myself</u> letting the amount of
people in my immediate circle of friends (homies)
dwindle down. Friendship simply isn't the
same anymore, and that's okay. Our loyalty
doesn't have to change consistency for us to
re-appreciate good people in our lives.
Questioning the motives of the people supposed
to be motivating us? Take a step back. Re-evaluate
their intentions. They are not perfect and they
don't have to be, but the amount of honesty and
energy that you've applied to their lives needs to
be reciprocated.

MANNERS
&MEMORIES

Wish my appreciation levels never go down, and my ambition never goes away. Hoping all my homies know how much I appreciate them, and that they never go away.

SPONSORED BY HEAVEN.

Thankful for people that don't need to ask
questions for you to give them answers.

Thankful for slim girls with fat booties in yoga pants.

Thankful for moments of silence that sound loud.

Thankful for hot showers and
hot Cheetos.

Thankful for the good people that stick around
longer than needed, just to show you're needed.

Thankful for learning love before learning lust.

Thankful for friends that feel like family.

CROWDED
CALENDARS

Been looking around a lot lately. Not at people, but at their actions. How they talk. How they laugh. How they care more or care less about each other. Been looking around at their gestures and gentleness, their kindness and concern. But also their cruelty and corruption. Been looking around lately at how they all have time for themselves, but rarely have time for each other.

SOBER
STUBBORNNESS

Trust issues grow stronger the more our generation grows older. It's hard to have faith in someone who doesn't have faith in themselves. Everybody feels scared. Instead of living we're improvising our fears and letting go of the people that care. The love that's offered our way never finds us because we hesitate on accepting anything real. That's a problem. Because that mindset becomes contagious. It spreads. Two emotionally damaged people meet. They confuse lust with love, and their pride turns into pain. They lose sense of their lives and end up being hurt not from valid reasons but because their pride couldn't be put away for progress.

ASKING FOR
LIFE.

chapter thirteen

Dear _____ ,

There will always be a place in my heart for
the pain you are going through in your life. I
don't know if you're seeking help or attention
but regardless my compassion overwhelms my
concern and I have read your letters. I think not
taking your medication will be the worst thing for
you. I understand the feelings of the medication
might not be ideal but balancing your mind is
something that might give you peace. I know all
about the cutting, and you hurting your self. I
am hoping (and praying) that it does not escalate
into suicide. This letter will be short so you can
feel the sincerity and severity of my words. I want
more for you than you want from yourself. I have
believed in your abilities for awhile. I understand
your flaws but also understand your intuition. I
hope one day you find the peace and love that your
mom, friends, and family were not able to share.

Sincerely,
Somebody that wants you to get home safely.

WAIT, HOLD ON, WAIT.

Patience. That has always been a tough word/world for me. One can learn patience when he/she waits for a bed in a hospital because of overcrowding from patients. Patience, minutes don't have to be moments if what you've needed has been worth it all along.

TOGETHER WE'RE
BETTER

The more I read, and the more I pay attention
the deeper sense of pain hits my heart when I
understand the cruelty some people experience on
a human level. Little girls under 16 getting raped,
families torn apart to never be reunited again
because of war, dirty drinking water, famine,
greed, sickness, etc. The severity of our system
has become so severe that being homeless and
being home don't even have the same meaning
anymore. People are more worried about finding
money than finding memories. That's the hardest
thing for me to come to reality with. People's
consideration for other people's progress in life
diminishes as our age increases. Little kids have
the purest hearts because their childhood will be
based on momentary enjoyment that sets the tone
for their daily emotions. Our emotions are based
on extreme circumstances boosted by a society
firing 50 caliber bullets at our mental existence.
We can't find happiness because we can't find us.
My skin color, eye color, hair color, might not
match the worlds but my will to change it needs to
be as strong as the people giving up on us.

That if people learn blind love, and educated trust
that we can help each other, help each other.

I might not know your name but take my hand.
Let's create positivity.

CLEAN DISHES

The glass isn't half empty or half full. The glass has become dirty due to all of the hands grabbing to check how much has been left.

TALK **TO ME**

chapter 17

Being concerned and being curious when it comes to someone's well being are things that our generation has misguided. People ask questions to get answers, instead of asking questions to find more solutions. Your mental health and someone's mental help should meet a few times weekly to gain progress. It's important to speak mental, physical, and emotional health into people so they live longer and not just exist.

HEARTS VS
OLD QUESADILLAS

<u>Wasted time will always</u> be worse than wasted
money. That's why ex-relationships bother you
more than leftovers going bad.

BREAKING NEWS:

Victoria Secret models are getting skinnier and
skinnier every year. Hard to take a beautiful girl
out to eat when she won't.

HELP ME, **HELP YOU**

<u>Finding new ways to</u> appreciate the people that
have shown effort from the start. Those people
that pick up the phone whenever a ride is needed.
That answer your calls late at night. That buy
your meal when your wallet is forgotten. That
share time when your patience is lost. That find
ways to find your happiness when its misplaced
somewhere in life.

YOU SEE?

Blind patriotism ruins countries. Blind hatred
hurts hearts. Blind compassion saves children.
Blind anger rips souls. Blind passion confuses
minds. Blind love keeps us warm.

YOU CAN'T FIND US

Let's get lost. Let's drift into a random forest, in a random part of the world, in a random time zone with random people. Let's meet people that speak different languages, different cultures and different intentions on why they decided to get lost with you. Let's mentally start over. Let's physically get better. Let's emotionally grow stronger. Let's get lost.

CATCHING **FATE**

He's chasing her, she's chasing him, he's chasing her because she's chasing him. The cycle.

3AM APOLOGIES

Forgive me. I didn't mean to love you at a bad time. I didn't mean to hold your heart when I had no intention to hold your hand. I didn't mean to feel your body with no desire to feel our future. Forgive me. I made a mistake. I became scared so my flaws came out. I became insecure about caring more than my conscious. I broke your heart and I'm still forgiving myself.

RESERVE WHAT YOU **DESERVE**

chapter 25

<u>People deserve respect</u> and consistency. People deserve somebody to believe in you when you don't believe in you. People deserve patience. People deserve inspiration. People deserve productivity. People deserve empathy. People deserve positive energy. People deserve people to give you the time of day to hear how your day went, any time of day. People deserve powerful hand shakes you can feel in your wrist and hear in their voice. People deserve intellectual conversations where the topic will never be other people but always ideas on how to add to the progress.

CC: LIFE CLASSES

College isn't the best years of life. Random nights spent with friends that feel like family in random places added up are the best.

See chapter 38

LETTER TO MY
SON

One day if I have a son I want to teach him. I want
to teach him honesty. I want him to know that
his word will be his bond and that by reaching
out with the truth to everyone he can create a
more genuine life. I want to teach him respect.
Everyone he meets won't be the same as him,
like him, or even respect him. He doesn't have
to follow in their footsteps. Showing respect
in any scenario will help him help others. I
want to teach him empathy. Caring. Genuinely
caring about other people will help him keep
his priorities focused on the right things, at the
right time. I want to teach him to treat women
better. Our society (myself) included has taken
the women that have birthed, cared, sheltered,
and loved us for granted. We wait for mothers day,
to exclaim our love in anyway. I want my son to
do better then I have done. I want to teach him
hard work. That the amount of effort he gives in
anything should never go down. That the only
thing stopping him is him. That his consistency
in effort determines what he will get out of life.
I want to teach him forgiveness. People, things,
and scenarios harming the ones he loves does not
justify him living in bitterness and anger for the
rest of his life. Learning to forgive will help him
re-learn to live.

SETTLERS

chapter 29

Momentary gratification opposed to anything
long term and substantial. Pick wisely.

BACK IN THE **DAY**

chapter 30

<u>People learn the most</u> from some old folks. Not because their age defines their knowledge but because they have experienced enough events in their lives to form opinions on almost anything. They have a deeper understanding of work because they've been forced to work most of their lives. They have a deeper sense of love because they've either been in love or searched for love for many years. They have a deeper outlook on the youth. Because they have been young, older, and are now old. Some of these people have a deeper sense of family. They don't know how much longer they have to live so they would rather spend time & money making memories with friends & family than themselves. Listening to old folks tell their memories sometimes becomes deeper because of how long they've been holding onto them. It's easy for us to tell friends what we had for lunch yesterday, its harder to describe what dress she was wearing while walking down 2nd street in 1947.

DAY DREAMS

chapter 31

Day dreaming never seemed like a waste of time to me. Mentally preparing my ambition like Thanksgiving dinner. See even though I was staring into empty space I was able to rearrange knowledge, beliefs and morals in my head. I was able to break down understanding and reevaluate situations. Day dreaming will only be wasted if you're dreaming about your day being wasted.

WORKING ON **YOU** TIME

chapter 32

Spending time alone has become under
appreciated in todays society. It allows moments of
clarity when you're caught up in a daily lifestyle.
People get scared when they're by themselves for
too long. They begin questioning their self worth
and evaluating what they add to society. But that's
the wrong way too look at it. The wrong way in
my eyes at least. These brief (usually) moments of
alone time allow us to put the things that matter
back into perspective.

WANT MORE

Accepting less then you deserve in anything will hurt your future. See people these days accept less when it comes to their education but still think they deserve more opportunity. People accept less in their relationship but still think they will receive trust. People accept less when it comes to their declining health but still refuse to change their diet. Once we stop accepting less in these different aspects of our lives we will be able to accept more of what we deserved in the beginning.

REALLY

Sometimes I create mental stories in my head to understand people better. Here is one of those stories. "I never had time. Even when I was with her I was looking at my watch. That created arguements. "Stop! Watch me instead of always looking at your watch!" I calmly put my hands over my eyes. I hated to watch her get mad more then she hated me watching my watch. 5, 10, 15 minutes go by... We were almost late. Owning a car that goes 0-90 in 6 seconds doesn't matter when my wife never looks at the time. See I always used to look at my watch so we weren't late. But she has Alzheimer's now. She doesn't remember my face, the time, or where we're going. I never watch the time anymore. I don't even own a watch. I don't care about being late. I just watch her and enjoy the time we have left."

DON'T STOP

Feeling alone while going through something becomes worse then what ever you're going through. That's why it's important to talk to people that are concerned for your wellbeing and not just curious.

I PROMISE TO BE

chapter 36

People think about others even those others aren't
thinking about people.

LETTER TO MY
DAUGHTER

chapter 37

One day if I have a daughter she's going to make
me smile a lot. She'll make me smile because
of her carefree attitude. She's make me smile
because her presence will always be powerful.
That her dreams, desires, and aspirations in
life will be something I constantly look forward
to hearing about and watch grow. She'll make
me smile because she'll show me how to re-
appreciate the little things in life. Her first
steps, her first words, her first laugh will all have
a deep impression on my life. It will make me
thankful and realize that i've grown up to learn
to appreciate someone as much as I appreciate
myself.

CHAPTER 38:

Chapter 27 is blank because there are still too
many parts of my life that I don't understand by
any means. These things I have stopped trying
to understand and have learned to simply accept,
putting my mind at ease. Chapter 27 is the most
important chapter in this book because it relates
to everybody. Everybody has a blank page in the
book that is there life that they try to fill. They
might fill this blank page with, money, drugs, sex,
work, working out, ect but the page will always go
back to being blank. Instead of filling this page in
your life accept 2 things. Right now you're where
you're supposed to be in life. Improving your life
daily continues to be an option.

PACIÊNCIA

chapter 39

Dear Dad,

I know I haven't been the best son. I know you
haven't always been around. I know that my anger
isolated us from each other for years. I know that
learning forgiveness helped me heal. I hope one
day you're proud of me.

Sincerely,

Benjamin.

ACKNOWLEDGEMENTS

Thank you to Twait, Sheldon, Sundermann, Hastings, Yeakey, Noffsinger, Town & the countless other people that have inspired/ helped me put my words onto paper.